Contents

Look at the sky..........2
Read the colour..........3
Read the sun...............5
Read the clouds.........6
Read the moon........10
Read the night sky...14

2 Look at the sky.

Look at the colour.

If the sky is blue, the sun is shining.

If the sky is grey, the sun is behind the clouds.

If the sunrise is pink,
bad weather is coming.

If the sunset is pink,
good weather is coming.

Look at the clouds.
Look at the colour.

If the clouds are white,
it will stay dry.

If the clouds are grey,
it may rain.

Look at the clouds.
Look at their shape.

If they are moving quickly, the wind is blowing.

If they are moving slowly, the air is still.

Look at the moon.
Look at its shape.

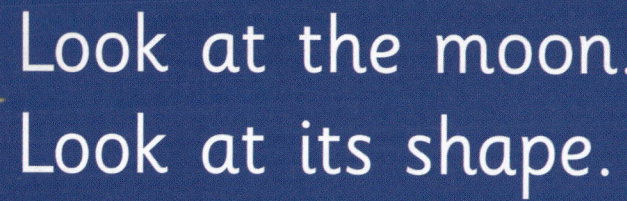

If the moon is round, you can see it all.

If the moon is thin, you can only see part of it.

Look for these in the day.

Look for these at night.

Glossary

Forked lightning

Full moon

Comet

Half Moon

Rainbow

Stars